crimes of the
dreamer

also by naomi ruth lowinsky:

The Motherline: Every Woman's Journey to Find Her Female Roots

red clay is talking: poems

a maze: poems

crimes of the dreamer

poems
by

naomi ruth lowinsky

i caught the dream
and rose dreaming
— H.D.

Scarlet Tanager
BOOKS

Cover art: Christine Brennan, "Girl with Bowl and Bird"
(Image first appeared on the cover of *Psychological Perspectives*, #38, Winter 1998-1999)

Back cover photograph: Gretel Lowinsky

Cover design: Andrea DuFlon

Book design: Scott Perry

Typography and composition: Archetype Typography, Berkeley, CA

Published by Scarlet Tanager Books
P.O. Box 20906
Oakland, CA 94620

Library of Congress Cataloging-in-Publication Data:

Lowinsky, Naomi Ruth
  Crimes of the dreamer : poems / Naomi Ruth Lowinsky.
      p. cm.
  ISBN 0-9670224-8-7
  I. Title.

PS3562.O8962C75 2005
811'.54--dc22

          2005002777

acknowledgments

Some of the poems in this collection have appeared or are forthcoming in the following publications:

American Writing: "lady of Florence, again"
Asheville Poetry Review: "comes someone's music"
Baybury Review: "dream of origin," "the woman you're not"
DAYbreak: "if you follow the track of the dream"
Dark Moon Lilith: "it must have been you," "Ursula"
Edgz: "this strange practice," "beyond the pale," "how poetry is born"
Heaven Bone: "in her chair," "in the real story"
International Dream Quarterly: "separate darknesses" (published as "labyrinth")
Pagan's Muse: Words of Ritual, Invocation, and Inspiration (Citadel Press):
　　　"pantoum for a witch's sabbath"
Psychological Perspectives: "mystery"
Rattle: "letter to a first analyst" (nominated for a Pushcart Prize in 2002)
Small Pond: "crimes of the dreamer," "i am the word"
Tar Wolf Review: "becalmed"

for Betty

and Gareth

who showed me the way

contents

crimes of the dreamer

follow the track of the dream

i asked for a dream

and because you coughed in the night
i remembered
the fire
painted by the woman
who had been through it all—

                        her testimony to the ones who burned—

she mixed her own
colors
red with just the right yellow

                    for the blaze

green with a touch of purple

                    for foliage
                    violet for the pretty horses
                            our flesh sacrifice   O

                            the leaping flames to god

you turned in bed and groaned about what
                        you wouldn't remember—

the woman who painted fire in my dream
                    held it up for me
                        to see through

3

if you follow the track of the dream

from life to life   one planet blending into another   in the company of the man
who reads stone   maybe you'll find yourself
                            on a boat in the ocean   chasing a whale

or in the middle of the woods   startled by a fox with turquoise teeth
he grins at you   then dashes off into the undergrowth

maybe you'll follow its spoor to a bear fast asleep on your living room rug
in the middle of whose dream you are beating your head against flesh walls
                propelled through bleeding lips into

                                                    yet another dream

softly now   the man who reads stone has a message for you

                    god's will is not the fruit you longed for!
so what if you've been visited by a finger-pointing prophet   blessed by an elephant
                walked up river to the original spring

                                                    even so
the yellow leaves lament their first green burst
and the old woman   whose name means wolf
                                    is waiting for you
                                            in the dark
                                                of the cave

sleep

i am crawling around the edges of you
                         longing for you
                                    sweet sleep
             that my grandson fell into this evening
             as i walked him and sang
             and his head hung heavy
                           on my arm

sleep
why do you hold yourself back from me
you were my first love
you wrapped me up in my mother's dark
knew me before i knew light
filled me with all i've become

            sleep
                my oldest familiar
               open your doors to the streaming stars
                       let lions loose to dance in the sky
                         and those who are gone
                                            let them return
                                          to speak my name

                     for everything that's lost
                                      is found in you
                    and everything changes
                                      its shape

rock becomes a giant lizard
           flame leaps from the rock
                        becomes word
                            becomes snake
                                becomes backbone
                                            mine!

sleep
only you can wash away
              the day's bile
this one i'm arguing with
that one who rubbed me
              the wrong way

              lead me down into your secret pools
                            rub oils into my body
                            take my muscles in hand
                            and smooth them out

                                    O sleep
                            lay your big blue weight
                                    upon me!

separate darknesses

i string my own pearls down the tunnels of night
i follow my own thread

sometimes in the night you moan
your body makes the gestures
of a story you've not told

sometimes in the night i dream
you and i are together
excavating old churches

i tell you dreams like this
you laugh

briefly we cross
making the pelvic gesture
of infinity
all ends and all beginnings
all tears and laughter pass
through the narrows
of our joining

then we fall back
into the separate darkness
we each enclose   and

i am alone again
with you

marriage

in my dream you give me two necklaces
        one of dark blue crystal
        surrounding a pendant in the shape of a woman
        the other of some cunning metal
            catches the red queen dancing

as in our long wed bed you bring her out of me again
              and again

        in the same dream i am wandering around
        looking for my lost penny loafer
        from when i was sixteen

and in the same bed   we lie exhausted
        filled with unbearable stories

            the old moon wanes

i sit alone   wearing the dark blue necklace
        our lady of silences   blue for sky
            blue for sea
            blue for what gathers in me

        the red queen   she will return
            shoes will be lost and found
            in my dream

        and in yours
        a beautiful woman
        presses her breasts against you

i wake to question the night

what are you stirring in me!
some cup of zero!
you have ladled out too many dreams
even a sleeping bear cannot digest them—

> the well dressed angel
> in a bad part of town
> who says it is time

> someone important
> has painted a tree made of words
> whose roots go down
> > below down

> whose tongue is in my ear!
> whose hand is shaking   my heart!

cradle rock me back
to the sleep of where

> > i began

> be my dark
> cooking vessel
> stew for tomorrow
> > > my bones

crimes of the dreamer

what can it mean when the dream
sends you off to some
russian backwater–
a summer house
guests in white linen–
the host takes your arm
with a nasty laugh
he says:
"everytime I dream of you
i commit a crime!"

you say: "what crime?"
then think better of it
"no, don't tell me anything
i don't want to be accountable
for what you do."
"the hell you don't" he says
"its your dream
we're in!"

where was he lurking
all the years before
you dreamt him?
did he believe
in the revolution?
was he a member
of the party?
did your father's
father know him
before he stole himself
and all of you who followed
out of the country

under a bale of hay!
this undigested
piece of a cossack is taking up
too much space
in your imagination

"then what *do* you dream about me?"
you ask your intrusive host
you know he expects you to
its how you earn your strange
american living

"i dream you are driving
a big red car
i get in i say 'move over
i'll take the wheel!'
or i dream you are making love
with your american husband
who has a polish father
on a king size mattress
with lots of pillows
you are making sexual noises
i lust after you
lust makes me do things

i pull off a trick or two
in the underworld
i get rich
i buy a summer place
invite guests—
you come
in *your* dream
to *my* house

now *you* tell me what
                                it means—"

becalmed

"don't go chasing whales" she sd
meaning that i am a small human
                    on a boat
                    the ocean is huge
                    full of wandering   sea horses
                                    castles of coral   prickly
                                                              sea urchins

i sit in white mist
          faintly rocking
when will the wind come up?

                    i think i am travelling east
                          toward sunrise
                                    when the black mouth closes down on me   says

                                        "you're going
                                              where i say
                                              you're going!"

a whale's tongue
is a great soft cushion
                a whale's throat
                is a long tunnel

                    i sit in some god's
                                    great dark—

                                        awaiting
                                              what?

labyrinth

This is internal labyrinth of Nuit
her bowels
thru which stars fall to birth

— *Diane di Prima*

we're talking large intestine
        whale story

           Humbaba's murky domain—

           in the middle of the creature with two mouths
           you see   no light

           guts don't work
           you throw up compulsively

                      birth place
                          severed
                    from your food source

                    we're talking binge eating
                    30 years of notebooks
                    dreams
                        poems
                            arguments

who will enter here and find
           the thread?

when you're tunneling through
the belly of the beast

sunlight has nothing
to say

dawn is

a last glimpse
of great white owl feet—

        flashes of a dream—
          a pregnant wolf
          lavender roses arranged
                in green bottles
                before a mirror—

a dove whose soft gray underfeathers
tickle the dream of the man in her bed
he rustles his feet and murmurs—

dawn is
turning over
        fragments—
              fights with her love
              pieces of a dirge

          this sweet
              wing sweep of light
                    stroking her
                        eyelids

past tense

how can something have to wait until tomorrow
      and then turn into   yesterday?
           asked the child
           in the old woman's dream

it seemed to take forever
sitting on that egg
      and now
      the whole story–

           what hatched
           what flew away
           what pecked at her heart
           whose white feather landed on the flower
           in the middle of her prayer rug

      is being written

           in the past
              tense

letter to a first analyst

I caught the dream
and rose dreaming
          — H.D.

he sat with me in the early years   when it was all
coming apart   my too young marriage   that business of the donkey
in the basement   the father whose eyes entered
me   took what they would

he sat with me   and i opened like a window
in a suffocating room whose drapes have been drawn for too long
                    now blinds snapped up   smell of hot tomatoes
                                        strawberries in the sun—

                                   i had been living in my body
as though it were an unmade bed   for years the smell of decomposing
dreams under the bedside table   crumpled kleenex   bad blood spotting
the sheets   the children were so little they wandered in
wanting their breakfast   and me just waking from a dream of spitting out my teeth
on the road or dream of using a contact lens for contraception it splintered
inside me   what spirit led me to him   after the terrible dream— my daughter's
head was severed from her body   my mother's voice said: "you'll never
                                        get her together again"

i write to tell him that i danced at that daughter's wedding   on a hillside in berkeley
not far from his house   she was beautiful   and i was glad   for
all the years of catching the morning dream   the hours he sat
with me   through sandstone storms and backdoor men   even death's most
yellow incarnation made a pass at my bed   but he
who opened windows   closed that door   i remember

17

once he told me the story of a prince   and a hairy wild man fresh out of the forest
they wrestled   for a long time   fought   until each knew
the other's   body and mind   until they were   inseparable
                                                                        friends

this strange practice

one chair
one couch
one talks to oneself
        in the presence of another–
                dreams come
                visitations from
                        the witch
                        her gathumping shoes
                                on the other side
                                of childhood–
                                also the wolf
                                his dinner table teeth

                        how can a quiet room become
                        a belly full
                                    of misery!

and she
her tongue
        gone wrong
            is now the one who
            (same old story)
            snicker snack your cut out heart
                        is dropped
                                  into a bag
                                        of shame until
                      next hour

one who was seen but not heard
                    pours out a belly full of ache—
one who can hear

            sends breath to belly

                    hot blood
                            to your heart

in the absence of the dream doctor

while you were gone
a bad mood snatched me
i fell into a place of mud
earth clung to me and would not let me go

my heart hurt
no one knew
my dreams scared me
no one knew
a good thing happened
no one knew
a bad thing happened
no one knew

while you were gone
babies were born
people got married
planes crashed
the owl hooted
a deer looked me in the eyes
for a long moment
one morning
at the bottom of the hill

while you were gone
that big bully girl
i've told you about
turned out to be your daughter
in a dream
you made her go away
you even made a fist at her
which was helpful

but even you don't know
what you did for me
in the dream

a little boy
had sewn himself into a pillow
he was suffocating
on goose down
swallowing chicken
feathers
until his big
red bearded brother
cut him out of there

a gnostic singer sits silent
by a huge blue glass aquarium
fish swim in it
(this happens in a dream)

while you are gone
an alchemist tells me
the treasure is in
the lower heaven
(this happens in a book)

while you are gone
red onions make
a joyful noise in my mouth
they burn in my gut
i put my ear to the belly of
the lower heaven
(this happens in my stomach)

you tell me there's a growth
in my navel

i need to have it checked out
right away
now what is that
supposed to mean

a self-devouring prophecy
in the place of chi
just as i was learning
to breathe
from my belly
letting the tired old reach
for outer glory
fall away
like the long red strips
of madrone bark
under which the new baby green flesh
is revealed

what am i supposed to do
with diagnostic information
that you give me
in a dream
while you are gone

i find a red fox
in a great crowd of people
he has a small mouth
just like the dental hygienist said
i do
only his is full of
pointy turquoise teeth
i want to stroke him
he wants to bite me

he says
he is the fast and tricky run
of my mind
the leap
the play
the disappearance into
the bushes
the quick brown fox
from learning how to type
is actually red
is actually fierce
has turquoise teeth

while you are gone
he runs back into
                              my woods

in her chair

SHE   in great heaven
turned her ear
to great earth
— Enheduanna

she combs through your dreams
braids your thoughts
ties a purple ribbon in them

                  remembering pieces of how
                       you came in

                       head of a girl
                       in a tower

                              foot stamping
                                 dwarf

              your grandmother's
                    lost silver

                          hands—

hour after hour she followed you
                into that storied dark

                      cave eyes
                    hollowed out ear
                            belly

                    tracking the fox
                          with turquoise teeth—

she was there
in her chair
when the great snake wandered away
from the center of the earth

25

your back went out
there was something wrong

with your guts

she was there when the bomb blew up
in the oven
she heard the howling

she was there
when the tower fell

and when the woman in a red sari
gold coins on her belly dancer's belt
tucked you into
bed
told you
the real story

in the real story

you are a dancing girl
a devadesi from the temple at Jaipur
or maybe it is Ur
the sacred fire's been lit
i've taught you how
to catch your own sweet pulse—

        you await the stranger
        who crosses the desert
                on a red mare
        two moons this night
        your hands on his back
        your soles on the stones
        you drink
                the milky way

        in the real story
        your open thighs reveal
                the crescent
                    moon

dream of origin

sprung
        out of the attic room
        out of the family house in Queens
        out of steerage—
        out of the coffin that washed up on shore

            brief laughter
                between my parents
                (they are young again
                wearing the elegant hats
                    of their time)

                    i sit between them
                    on a park bench—
                    all is forgiven—

            but i do not think they see
                        what lives
                            in dark waters

            that breathing pod of whales
                        watching

the woman you're not

she of the attic fire

of witch's oven
of seven lost clay tablets

     has become my familiar–

     who can say how
          this happened?

     that they unearthed her
     enigmatically smiling face
          at Troy?

     that she danced topless in a bar
          named Babylon
          singing Innana's vulva song?

     that she went bottomless into the pit
     riding the devil's hard knuckled cock

     that she was swallowed by the dragon
          or was it a whale?

     that it took her two times seven years
        to tunnel her way out
        to scrape lost syllables
           off the rocks
        to lure her tongue back
          from the cattails in the swamp

to translate

     what belly knows
     into words
     that can be said
     between two sitting women
           in a quiet room?

what got into her

                              came fluttering
out of the fallen animal furs
in her mother's closet
the persian lamb
the tired red fox still eating
its tail

tried to find a way into her
body
                    she was only
                    fourteen
                    bending to see
                    her own dark

                                with a hand
                                held mirror

took most of a life
time listening
to heart and lung pulses
soles of her feet portals
to the sky
lovers' tongues to know her
old
lost
secret

wrapped it around her
night robe of lore and language
animal skin
shroud
placenta
        opened her lung wings

33

and she dove
into the milky way
is drinking from

the deep sky

slave of willow, age 11

who struck her then
who wrapped her willow and
        serpent self
          around that girl's body
            slipping the hot pulse of sun into her ear
               making her a slave
       to how
        the smell of new cut meadow grass
     beats green the inside of her head and she
  belongs to rough bark
and what the river sings–

    her girl friend sharon
      (usually a wild horse
        or the queen of sheba)
         is now the high priestess
          of some cult of willow switch–
            what is that look in her eye
          parting weeping willow hair
      entering where

*   root knows*
*   the inside of the earth*
* the dark*
between her mother's thighs they say
* she comes from–*
*   jungle heat*
*   bullrushes*
*   rose of sharon*
*   a sudden crescendo of startled birdwings*
*   and she is*
*   released–*

(this is not a feeling
        she's supposed to have
                every evening
      her father so carefully places
    her hands outside
the covers)

O sweet goddess of dirt
    who slipped your knowing
        tongue into her then
           and now–
              that she is halfway home–

          remember her
          the always alphabet
             of trees
              of roots

it must have been you

sweet lord
who lured her into the long red suck of the topless bar
the smell of cheap champagne   it must have been you
made a temple of that shoddy North Beach scene
convention going men far away from their wives
how their dark suited crotches swelled
how glazed their eyes under her spell   she had never known the power
of her swinging breasts   her dancing feet   her hips before you
                                                                got into her

were you making up for that   so disappointing wedding night!
after the years of foreplay in the dark parked chevrolet
virginity was difficult to shake   you had to break it all up   the sweetheart marriage
whose other shoe was a coffin   sometimes she could barely breathe
sometimes she laughed so hard she cried   it must have been you
bad boy with a flute   saying 'pan is no longer dead'   playing 'hey Jude'
on the juke box and she—   just back from India where they never stopped
worshipping you—   was filled with the golden shower of your coming

it must have been you   stole her out of her married bed
in the topless bar they knew she didn't belong   'too passionate' they said
the other girls chewed gum   ground mechanical hips   the boss had short man's
disease   swore he'd nail every girl he hired   turned out to have the smallest cock
she'd ever met and trouble   keeping it up

it must have been you   snake in the summer grass who came to her open door
in the form of the editor   who first put her words into print
you stayed the weekend   were gone   and she was Dido
the poems came ranting   wailing   she cut off her hair   looked for

you everywhere   the supermarket   the poetry reading
yours was the ache   yours was the rending
yours the wild word in the night   sweet lord of the apple tree
                                        half a life later   she knows
                                                it was you!

betrayal

when you were not   what i thought you were
        and you wouldn't what you said you would
               i couldn't find my face
                 in your eyes
       and your hands
         that had shaped and sustained me
              dropped me

              into the great empty

something growled in the corner of the cave
      it had been licking wounds
           now it remembered teeth

          in some other country
          this never happens
          mother and daughter remain
             in the same house
             spitting out ragged canines

but here
    where you've broken promises
        rained acid
        soured milk

      something muscular happens
          between us
          something with fists and raised
               voices
          i am that i am what you aren't

            and i see your face
             for the first time

pantoum for a witch's sabbath

for leah

long ago when night was her familiar
she knew the moon and the moon knew her
i mean carnally
those stories about sex with the devil are about this

she knew the moon and the moon knew her
joy from the sky made a music in her body
those stories about sex with the devil are about this
moon penetration   stars awakening

joy from the sky made a music in her body
lion arose   horse flew
moon penetration   stars awakening
something from forever loved her for a night

lion arising   horse flying
roots of the tree reach up into the sky
something from forever loves her for a night
and the moon sings

roots of the tree reach up into the sky
branches touch down into earth
the moon sings
naked she is   and flying

branches touch down into earth
i mean carnally
naked she is   and flying
rooted in the night   her familiar

40

beyond the pale

these were the names of her parts:
forever yesterday maybe tomorrow   now

she remembers
          herself   heavy
                    with possibility
                         she lived in the home of a woman
                                   with glamour who threw back
                                                  her chestnut hair—

if she let the years fall away
             like the folds of a shawl
                        she'd be looking over water
                             at this very moon
                                      singing to Atthis

if she let the years fall away
                        she'd find the perfect fragment
                                of herself
                                lighting a fire
                                      in the temple
                                                 at Ur

she

she— she WHO she...?
                    — Judy Grahn

who is
    all magnetism
                    hot core
                    cold sky rock
                    bright mist veils her
                                    who spins
                                    the invisible
                                                    thread—
    blood rises to her
                    wheat yearns
                            for the cut
                                    of her scythe—
                                                    she—
                                    Ashera Sofia
                                    lady of all longing
                                                    lost to you
                                                            lifetimes ago—
                                                    appears to you now
                                                                    bearing
                                                                    clay
                                                                    tablets
how did we get to here
            from yesteryear?
                    birds ate
                    the trail of bread crumbs
                    and at the seventh gate
                            they stripped her
                                    lapis beads
                                    seed pearl crown

42

veil embroidered
            with the eyes
                        of snake—

do you remember?
you stood in the corner
            of the field
            an old woman's words in your ear?
            "go to his tent in the night
                        say nothing
                        lie down at his feet"

            O you were moon besotted
                        someone's red sea rant
                        took over your head
                              you hardly heard
                        the door shut
                                    behind you
                                    the key turn—

who will weep for her lost
                  lapis beads?
who will make a noise
            among the grave robbers?
            they have stolen the golden navel
                        of the world   her
                        old libation bowl's been sold
                        to decorate
                        some hedge fund manager's Manhattan
                                          penthouse—

43

fire within fire
whose shriek
in the attic?

                        whose knife slashes
                              your thumb?
                        whose quill pen is dipped
                              in your blood?

chaos lady

can't we go back to how it was before it all caved in?
before the diagnosis
　　　　　　the weeping
　　　　　　　　　　　the throwing up all over the bathroom floor?

　　　　　back to when there was summer
　　　　　and children calling from the lake?

　　　　　　　　　　　chaos lady
　　　　　　　　　　　on your way to bag lady
　　　　　　　　　　　　　　　who let you in?

you are the one i never wanted to become
hair so thin it can't find which way to curl
embarrassed protrusion of belly you are
　　　　　　　　　　　someone's ex-wife
　　　　　　　　　　　　　hanger on at the edges of the party

whale that swallowed my mother whole   took her to another country where
　　　　　　　　　　　　　　　i couldn't find her—

long ago you sent me to my bed   i thought i'd recovered but here you are
walking in through the front door
　　　　　　　　　　chaos again
　　　　　　　　　　come to steal our thunder
　　　　　　　　　　the light out of our eyes

you've changed are self assured   big of hips
you bring a pretty basket full of hissing snakes
　　　　　　let them loose on the chinese rug!
　　　　　　　　　　snake in the bed—
　　　　　　　　　　snake in the pantry—
　　　　　　　　　　snake under the floorboards poised to strike the baby—

chaos lady
     on your way to bag lady

         you've broken our promise
         smashed our holy images
         torn the roof off the temple to expose us
                 to the dangerous sky

         i sit on a yellow velvet chair
            try to rise above
               your assault

         you slap me down

         "earth to earth" you say,
             "ashes to ashes!"

"the stone is an orphan"

your many devoted
who will be burnt
like sun–scorched fire bricks
                    — Enheduanna

if i am no longer turned to your face

if i am just this hard moon stone
scratched by a stick   flame comes most of the time
the wind the sun the rain move me and the story
simply happens or doesn't like the gray fog pours over the western hills
                                        your face fades away like the river
                                                                    delta

it is summer   we are going to italy
an old friend is dying   grandchildren who will be born
cousins are drifting in their lovely mothers wombs   dreaming
their sea changes we have seen their tiny white bones   floating
                                                    in darkness

47

lady of Florence, again

the river
your hand on the small of my back
me crossing the old bridge—
> you burst through the gates of my eyes
> light up the back of my skull

> spinal column i rise to greet you
> praising Maria in white marble
>   you open the wings of my lungs
> know the way down to my guts
>> your gravity sinks
>> below stones

i know you in my every breathing cell
but i can't find your face
or a picture of me on your lap as a child
> why don't you run up and greet me
> whirl me around like a girl before time spits me out!

---

it's not about a snapshot   a map   or the color of my eyes
its about a bird that sings in the inner courtyard
an old bridge you keep crossing
how seven blue statues of truth are aligned across oceans
in your dream—
> *from Italia to the lady*
> *with a torch in New York harbor........*

---

no one knows us in this town we are ghosts visiting
half-lit memories we have a perfectly
adorable make-believe life—
                    our apartment requires toilet paper
                                        milk for tea—

we have taken a train to the city on water   gold light   winged lions
returned 'home' through a narrow causeway
out of the dream city   fancy lady city   harlequin city   hustler city
to the city of our lady of the white flower—

we are caught in underwater reflections   cross currents
the sudden storm that blew the waves backwards

                                                    up river
somewhere in the dark waters is the ghost of a day—

                    we are so fleeting to ourselves
                    walking down a narrow street
                    catching a glimpse of where
                    we bought the flowered umbrella
                    saw the white figures standing on the hilltop
                                        like wordless gods—

----

a lady is giving music lessons in the church
a stone woman is holding the body of her son
we light a candle
we light a candle

i ask you
do you know the river rat
swimming through the arches of the Ponte Vecchio?
do you know the broken old lady   her begging bowl
crumbled in the doorway of the church?

49

you tell me
liquid gold is created in the hollow caverns
of your body
face of the dark
Christ is etched into the back
                          of your skull–

---

last night our lady of Florence was in the church Orsan Michelle
tired face of Anne   mother of Mary   the baby Jesus on her knee

                I am the broken heart of your truth
                                    the lost tooth–

our lady was wearing a flowing black gown
had a long roman profile   dark eyes
played the viola in three of Bach's Brandenberg concertos
or she was the henna haired flirt on the violin
in tight velvet slit above her knee
beckoning her admirers closer

this morning she is wiping clean
the windows with green shutters
of shops on the Ponte Vecchio–

lovely lady none of this comes easily
the streets are full of secret juices   humid bodies
vacant men with cardboard signs proclaiming
their hunger–

                we take your photograph
                eat your eggplants soaked in olive oil
                bite into the tart abandon of your artichoke hearts–

50

in shop windows   in blue robes on the sides of churches
skirt slit above the thigh   gold frizzled on your head
wearing a hat   not wearing a hat
in the Piazza d'Annunziata—

                    (the muttering priest in the church
                    the miracle of how you appeared
                    kneeling women   lit candles
                          golden rays entering your ear—)

our lady reveals herself
in displays of purple radicchio   red strawberries
she flows in water under the arches of the old bridge
rides a Vespa   her flowered summer dress blows up showing dark thighs
she bargains with me in the clothing store

take me home with you in this soft silk   this gauzy gray
stick me in your new leather bag with many compartments—

---

a voice says:
'we need to inform you that the garden is closing'

                    in the Piazza del Duomo
                    three tall young Africans
                    are selling reproductions—
                          elongated blue Etruscans,
                                (grave figures)

                                  waving goodbye......

Ursula

we who are bodies
of water   vessels of blood
secret cloisters where wild birds warble
little bears   big dippers
    in an ocean of dreaming

see each other's flaring spirits
across a table on a hillside
            overlooking Florence

(there was an Ursula when i was young
we had a cave together–
hid out from her leonine mother
under a red velvet comforter)

now
most of our elders
are gone
we ourselves are not
so young any more

you show me the prehistoric posture
of the shaman becoming
a bear
feet firm
on the ground
knees bent
head thrown back to see–
            ursa major

moonsong

swing low

        you
        moon
           over me

                 pieces of you
                       come shining–

          * * * * * * * * * * * * *
          moon over the Ganges
          you took me when i was young
          showed me how the blue god dances

     * * * * * * * * *
sister moon
i slept in a field
with a man i didn't love
          but O

                 the mountains
                 the mountains and you!

       * * * * * * * * * * * * * * *
egg moon
purse full of babies
children chasing waves
dog at their heels and me–
                 labyrinth of sea sand & shells

* * * * * * * *

moon mad
        comings and goings untethered
            some goddess hung
               on a meat hook
                  and me
                    empty my measure of mother
                       dry as a rattling gourd
                          in winter
                  *

O half bitten apple moon
            you
              peer at me through weeping
                 willow hair
                      where
                  a girl first felt
                      green fire

* * * * * * * * * * * *

creature moon
  come to bed–
             husband of many years
             sniff out my lust and longing
             give tongue to nipples and thighs
                     and i–
             your moment of flesh–

                swing low to your love
                    'til snake rises
                      stone sings

full moon before her birthday

she stands in the dark
by an open window
most of the moon has been
                    drained out of her

                              poured into the goblet sky—
                              if she could tip her head back
                              drink the dark light
                                   could she swallow it again
                                        from the beginning?
                                        the tongues in her ears?
                                        the mouths at her breast?

there comes an end
to possibility
some babies must die
a man is given the task
of carving a triangular handle
                         to swing shut a door
                         say its done
                                   its over—

she is full of contention
she wants to argue about what's hiding
                         in the back of the closet
she has been to India
and seen the little fire maiden dancing
                              on hot coals—

if the moon were the tip
of a silver needle
tying this life
              together

instead of some old power house
of a sky rock
demanding reflection

if the moon were a single pearl
on her neck
on the day of her wedding
instead of an empty goblet of wishes

if the moon were the light
at the end of the tunnel

god's mouth saying NOW!

could she suffer herself
to be born again
into this rocky
vulva?

snake and stone story

like the FIRST SNAKE
i come out of the mountains
                    — *Enheduanna*

the story is
        unutterable
                magnetic—

                comes down from the mountains
                arises from the center of the earth
                        tugs at the soles of my feet
                        from under the stones at *sante croce*
                        from the roots of the willow at river's edge
                        from the base of my spine to the tip of the old
                                                snake brain—
                                                swan's neck arches

snake glides through the whole
meander   ties it all together like the needle pulling thread
                only i can't see the gleaming point
                why do you speak to me in mysteries!

                                unspeakable mouth of the underworld
                                        tell me your stone stories—
                                        what got burned
                                        what broken into a thousand pieces
                                                casting out

the whole howling sacred circle— oak tree blue stone sun cycle dark of the moon
i want my grandmother's loch ness treasure   her basket of snakes
                                        her sea chest   engraved with
                                                your old wild
                                                        name

57

the woman you're not

is sure of her great
breasted body
mermaid to this one
siren to that   she knows

           where to put her feet   knows

                      each step

                          of the dance
          and her voice   from the deep

                      of her belly
          how she flings it about

                  like her long fiery hair
          her laugh that collides

                  with the stars

fear never touches her
whose dreams rise up like sap

         and any man who knows her knows her teeth

             and the back of her hand

         she grows crystals

              at the bottom of your garden
        wears purple silk and lavender chiffon
        travels in a green and yellow covered wagon
            drawn by seven giraffes

this morning in a dream she's handed you an image
        under glass   a bale of hay
          in a field of darkness

               burning

i am the word

i am the word

of your early morning mind   i say: linger awhile   let your tongue know
the taste of late november   the secrets of downhill houses   inner thigh of the ridge
dark firs   animal dreams—

listen: the word is a diamond pressed out of old coal
the mountain is an ear and the word is your spine
stretched and gleaming in the warm house

don't say you have no time for me today   i am your joy chariot   your worry wagon
your engine to the corners and the ends   i bring you word of the old lady
her fractured vertebrae   how do you move her out of assisted living
to the convalescent hospital?   how will she get word to the other ladies
who sat with her meal after meal discussing their gods?

i bring you word of the young women   carrying babies   trouble in their bodies:
cervical dysplasia   acoustic neuroma

i bring you word of the thanksgiving poet who showed up years ago in a dream
spreading his arms like wings   like a crucifixion   like the lover you took
when you fled your first marriage   word of what aches in your heart
in the old woman's back   in the young woman's cervix
in the leap of his body that lights up the back of your mind

word of your left shoulder aching   word of the blue spruce sending down roots

abandon all others and stay with me   play with me
don't leave me muttering to myself
while you get into your red car and drive to work

i am chanting the word that calls out a god
i am shaping your brain in the image of the word:

61

cow
moon
milk
sun
blood
vessel
young woman
old woman

word for what owl does on your tongue
word for what tree does to the back of your brain
word in the middle of the night
wakes you like a cat who wants to be fed
word for his hand on your belly
descending to the site of arousal
word for what is awakened–
has been for a thousand generations–
code twisting back to the old pelvic bones–

        the same thrust and gasp–
                animals do it–
                    dark code
                    before the word

how poetry is born

the word climbs out of the sea
where there have been so many
      in and out of each other's bellies—

            'thing' words
                salmon   sea snake   shark
            'color' words
                blue   red   magenta—
            'action' words
                swim   leap   devour
            words that make pictures
                of what mind can't sort—

              Aphrodite made of Cronos' genitals
                   out of Metis   our salt sea mother

                       ma   mare   she who gives refuge to the god
                                   Dionysos
                                   before she gets swallowed
                                         by Zeus

and the word climbs out of the sea
     shakes itself dry like an old sea lion
          sorts itself out   it is word
                              not root
                              not mother
                              not sea lion's whiskers
but inside our word is
            all wet
            80% water
            Metis   old salt brine of creation
                is spit out on dry land—

                  word becomes song
                      goes raving into the mountains

a poet's complaint about possession

out of chaotic dreams and early morning fragments
she tries to weave a story of where she is
lost to the old form   the circle with certain compass
there's a rip in the sky and chaos is pouring through

aspects of self she thought she knew   old friends
guides   inner companions   she's given them names
are tearing her up   into quarreling pieces of soul
they make conflicting demands   give unasked for advice
fight over their claims to her heart   the shape of her mind

Sophia for instance the mother of all matter
the light before sun's birth   breath before the word
it's her opinion the only fire worth tending
is the one that burns at the very center of earth

Stephen Dedalus shows up in a dream   cultivating crystals
so many faceted shapes and glowing colors
he argues for profusion confusion delight of the senses

there's an alchemist   on the other hand   in a state of frustration
he mutters "this stone is no stone"   and what can it mean when they say
"i am the black of the white and the yellow of the red"

a priestess is haunting the steps of the temple of Isis
awaiting the stranger who'll make her his love of the night

and then there's that ecstatic Chassidic rabbi
who throws her up to god like a bride in a chair
singing the psalms and the song of songs

64

and the green one   blessed be he   who leaps at her out of the forest
what does she do with him   become a river   turn into a tree

and when the mountain   speaks   proclaims itself
the one true face of god   then shapeshifts
into great stone lizard   rock iguana   then what

there's a devil on a burning lake in blank verse
a woman in a peignoir   with coffee and oranges
any of these she could follow for a month of sundays
they'd tell her stories   sing her songs

how many parts of herself can she be true to
(Sophia keeps warning her about overstimulation)

all the poems that want to get written   can't

if she sticks to iambic pentameter   will she cohere
where is the vessel into which she can pour   this quarreling
cacophony of internal advisers   each demands to be heard
it gets to be absurd   she's becoming a veritable tower
                                                    of Babel

the rabbi says *her* Sophia is not what *he* means by wisdom
the priestess of Isis has been stood up by whom
the alchemist says there's a shitfaced dragon in his retort
Stephen Dedalus brings her another crystal   another faceted jewel

and she like the woman in the shoe   with too many children
imagines herself   alone
                                        spacious
                                                    empty

a leo prays

lion
be with me
your burning heart   your leap
                              of certainty
sun knows your body
ocean smells you coming
you are not divided against your fierceness
any more than is the turkey vulture
                  against his bone cleaning
                  the spider   against her web

so if i have teeth
if my heart is a big thing that beats
              if it burns for word of you
                              let me not be divided against such passion

some say we are made of fragments
                  we drift in and out
                  without core
                  no god the conductor
                  no imprint   no plan
                              nothing from forever visits the dream
                              nothing from tomorrow remembers
                                              the dead stag
                  no imprint   that coven of black vultures we startled
                                              cleaning his bones

O my animal soul

               let them not sever me   from you
                                      who are green and glowing
                                      whose eyes are burning coals

                                      who danced in the planets at my birth

                                              my life is
                                                    your keep!

angel of her fire

poem ending with a line from the Book of the Law

i have given you time to dream
fire at the edge of the woods
     i have sat on a rock and waited
         while you tended kitchen fires

i have padded through your dreams
        as lion
        as tiger
        once in a library of esoteric texts
        i almost devoured you
        i have shown you the fire a woman creates
         when she writes with her menstrual blood

        you have forgotten
        you have driven to work
         in your battered infiniti
         and listened to the news
         fire on the temple mount
         fire in the old city

    once i leapt out at you in a dark dream
        slashed your thumb

listen to me!
i am the angel of your fire
i've burnt my hebrew mark upon your thigh

    there's a ladder to the veil beyond the sky
    there's a train about to leave for Jerusalem

let go of fear and sad stories
                 ride me
                         your beast with the fiery mane

                         i invoke you
                         my scarlet woman
                         sweet bride of babylon
                                 "arouse the coiled splendour within you"!

mystery

this never happened but it always is
            — Salustius

something is gathering
      out of what ocean whispered
                        all night
                              to the rocks
      out of what was revealed
                              in the dark of the cave
      out of a place i've not yet been
                        but always am—

            woods where the old gods speak—

                  time arrives
                        bedraggled and luminous
                        here
                        in the Sheraton Sofia

animal claws under the hotel table
            are about to leap out the arched window
            onto the verdigris dome of the old church—
                        Sveta Nedalya—
                        where pigeons roost
                        upon whose steps the bride is
                        about to be kissed by a little girl
                                    bearing rosebuds

and in the museum
we have seen the Varna Necropolis
king who died four millennia ago
gold discs around his head

70

golden penis sheath
golden navel of the world

      and the bird-headed goddess
      whose name is Helena
      our own root vegetable

something is soon to be
          gathered
          in rolling blue mountains
                    that call themselves Thrace

broken cooking vessel
peak we couldn't climb
girl friend with glowing red hair
          i lost in a pocket of sobbing
             from childhood
             (when did she return?)

             we walk among muttering stones
             we are almost old

what mystery is it
       that what tore us apart
       remembers us back
       among springs and old groves
       on animal hooves and covered with grape leaves
       we are carried away to some mountain altar
               where

fire in the dark
drum beat of heart
quickening leap of the god–
        who never has been
            but always is–

        dances
        behind closed
          eyelids

what the high priestess says at the temple gates

do not seek admission here
if your world holds together
    and everything knows its place in your house
        if the four walls have never fallen upon you
           or the living room furniture floated out
               of a sunday afternoon
                  on the breath of some god

do not pester me with inquiries
or shine a light behind these veils
    if trees have never prophesied to you
        or deer danced among the white clay men
               in your back yard

do not disturb my meditations
     if your sky has never ripped open
         light cut you to pieces

          if your head's not been cra cked
             by the hooves
               of the bull god

            how can my mystery
              enter!

visitation

And there are days here where everything is sails and more sails,
even though there's no sea in Jerusalem, not even a river
Everything is sails: the flags, the prayer shawls, the blackcoats.....
                            — Yehuda Amichai

the angel of "never again" and "no more"
        crept into my bed
                he wasn't invited—
                        this angel smells sour
                        he wants to get close
                        says it's part of the deal—
                        (my heart is a fortification
                        i have locked each of the four gates)
        but an angel can fly
            an angel can leap to the top of a stone wall
                                        and see

the ones you used to be
the ones you might have been
                        have packed their bags
                        are boarding the train for Jerusalem
you will never be the poet of that city
singing of white sails where there is no sea
            and even your own gleaming city
                    with its fine towers   its elegant bridges
                                    has stopped singing your name

angel i thought there'd be time
for the doing and the undoing
that was before all hell broke loose
                    son lost in the underworld
                            never again
                                    what i thought was forever

"never say never"
they like to say in your country
as though Troy never fell!
but "never" happens—

                    don't misunderstand me
                        "never" reveals
                            what is—
                            stiff knees
                            brown spots on the backs of your hands—
                            then suddenly some bird calls
                                lifts up your eyes to the treetop
                                where the reborn sun makes its nest

angel
we sat in the longest night
it was an ancient vessel of transport
there was sweetness between us

when you awoke
i stood by your bed
telling you what you'd rather forget
someday   not so long from now
                    you'll be gone

                                    begone

                                                    be

                                                        gone

never again what your green eyes see
of the western hills and the winter fog
never again my voice   within you   singing

sun will arise without you
   frogs will return to the pond
      owl will hoot on the roof of this house

          that is yours

            no more
            no more

if it were about money i'd be driving a Jaguar
if it were about fame i'd have gone on Oprah

       instead it's about the days
       ordinary as the mountains
       it's about hanging out with this angel
       in his tent of every color
         pitched in the center
           of my heart

where goes her song

when the bright blue bay   the golden bridge are ripped from her eyes
when her face is lost to the gaze of the sun
where will her morning devotions go   who will sit on this wooden porch
ponder the inward valley   make marks on white paper

when her face is lost to the gaze of the sun
when the eye of the sky   has forgotten her name
who will ponder the inward valley   make black marks on paper
where goes her song   her lamentation   her prayer

when the eye of the sky has forgotten her name
will anyone read these words
where goes her song   her lamentation   her prayer
the eyes of her love with their yellow glint

will anyone read these words
where go Sofia   Jerusalem   Calcutta
the eyes of her love with their yellow glint
cities   temples   flesh   torn out of memories membranes

where go Sofia   Jerusalem   Calcutta
the eyes of that beggar   his shriveled up hand in Bombay
cities   temples   flesh   torn out of memories membranes
the red lotus   the butter ball   what she offered to Kali

the eyes of that beggar his shriveled up hand in Bombay
she will become whatever one is after breath
red lotus   butter ball   an offering to Kali
ah! she will miss how the morning light falls into the valley

77

when she becomes whatever one is after breath
where will her morning devotions go   who will there be on this wooden porch
ah! she will miss how the morning light falls into the valley
when the bright blue bay   the golden bridge are ripped from her eyes

comes someone's music

comes the unturned page comes the name comes the footstep
— W.S. Merwin

comes wild
   the word—
         who knows who
           blew it in—
              says it is
                ocean
                oars' creak
                gulls' cry
                     at sun's set—

comes a pulse
    knows it is someone's
           heart
           lungs
           liver
           spleen
           handclap of gypsies
           footstamp of bharat—
                natyam dancer

comes a certain music
    does not remember
              its name
              whose famous old song
                   has broken
                    and entered
                       this house?

                                        snatch of Sappho?
                                        murmur of psalmist?
                                        laughter of Miribai's lord?

comes the old story–
            night ripper–
            the one about

                        going down
                                    under
                        to visit her sister
                                        veil torn
                                        meat hook
                                        death's eye–

comes long
            silence–

            she says–
                        can be language–

                                    there's a music
                                    even down here

                                                spirit moves
                                                shades chant
                                                in her dream
                                                someone is singing

                                                            the sun
                                                                back

about the author

Naomi Ruth Lowinsky loves her day job. She is a Jungian analyst, and a member of the San Francisco Jung Institute. Like all analysts, she has spent many years in her own analysis. Toward the end of her second analysis she was flooded by poems about the analytic process. These form the core of *crimes of the dreamer*.

She is the Poetry Editor for *Psychological Perspectives*, a journal published by the Jung Institute of Los Angeles, and teaches "Writing as a Spiritual Practice" in many settings.

Her first book of poems, *red clay is talking*, was published by Scarlet Tanager Books in 2000. A chapbook, *a maze*, was published by Modest Proposal in 2004. Her poems have appeared in numerous literary magazines, and she has been nominated for a Pushcart Prize three times.

also from Scarlet Tanager Books:

Wild One, by Lucille Lang Day
poetry, 100 pages, $12.95

The "Fallen Western Star" Wars: A Debate About Literary California, edited by Jack Foley
essays, 85 pages, $14.00

Catching the Bullet & Other Stories, by Daniel Hawkes
fiction, 64 pages, $12.95

Visions: Paintings Seen Through the Optic of Poetry, by Marc Elihu Hofstadter
poetry, 72 pages, $14.00

Embrace, by Risa Kaparo
poetry, 70 pages, $14.00

red clay is talking, by Naomi Ruth Lowinsky
poetry, 142 pages, $14.95

Call Home, by Judy Wells
poetry, 92 pages, $15.00

Everything Irish, by Judy Wells
poetry, 112 pages, $12.95